WHAT WOULD THE FOUNDING FATHERS THINK?

A **YOUNG** AMERICAN'S GUIDE
TO UNDERSTANDING WHAT MAKES OUR
NATION GREAT & HOW WE'VE STRAYED

*To the Anderson Family —
God Bless America!*

WRITTEN & ILLUSTRATED BY
DAVID BOWMAN

PLAIN SIGHT PUBLISHING
AN IMPRINT OF CEDAR FORT, INC.
SPRINGVILLE, UTAH

ISBN 13: 978-1-4621-1061-2

Published by Cedar Fort, Inc., an imprint of Cedar Fort, Inc.
2373 W. 700 S., Springville, UT 84663
Distributed by Cedar Fort, Inc., www.cedarfort.com

Cover and page design by Danie Romrell
Cover design © 2012 by Lyle Mortimer
Edited by Melissa J. Caldwell

Printed in the United States of America

10 9 8 7 6 5 4 3 2 1

Printed on acid-free paper

To my wife, Natalie, and our own little "rising generation,"
Baylee, Kambria, Lydia, Caleb

Foreword

David Bowman is a great American and a true rarity among educators. He is a passionate defender of liberty who recognizes the importance of the US Constitution, why and how it has survived the test of time, how it defers to the primacy of the individual, and for what purpose this beautiful document limits the authority of those who represent the people. More important, he recognizes the ultimate source of our rights—namely God—and boldly asserts that only by maintaining a solid, unwavering foundation of family, individual responsibility, and allegiance to our Creator can we truly preserve the freedoms that all mankind was born to enjoy.

What makes David so unique is his uncanny ability to bring this message to our young people in a way that is fun, exciting, entertaining, educational, and inspiring. David is doing what George Washington told us had to be done to ensure the longevity of freedom, namely "communicating [the science of government] to the future guardians of the liberties of the country."

One of the most important lessons David teaches is the foundation of our great country. As you journey through this book, you will not spend time discussing what many think are the most important issues of the day, such as which political party has the best ideas or the lobbying efforts of various groups. Instead, any young person reading *Dude, What Would the Founding Fathers Think?* will experience timeless principles that transcend politics. David will take you on a fabulous journey of why America is great, what your responsibility is as a citizen, and what the Founding Fathers would do if they were here today. You will truly experience the spirit of the greats like Benjamin Franklin, James Madison, and George Washington. Indeed, you will find yourself even beginning to think just as they did as they pledged their everything to a cause that was so much bigger than themselves.

One part of this book that is particularly important to me is the reference to family. As a father of six precious children, raised together with my beautiful wife, we have committed our lives to teaching our children why the family structure is critical to freedom. It is within our families that the freedom experiment begins and where we learn how to govern. As we are successful in governing within our families, so will we govern more effectively in our communities across the nation. The family structure is indispensable to a free society.

After all is said and done, what America needs today is young people of courage. America needs children who understand why our founding fathers pledged their lives, their fortunes, and their sacred honor, and what it means to do the same today. America needs young adults who understand what is truly at stake in this fight for freedom and government restraint on power. America needs the hearts and minds of all us to stop paying lip service to our Constitution and work tirelessly to return this country to its true destiny. Indeed, *Dude, What Would the Founding Fathers Think?* will inspire our rising generation to recognize why they should be proud to be an American and will move them to action.

I have only scratched the surface of the many great virtues of this important and profound work. This book provides the much-needed message that our young people must hear. And it is why I am absolutely honored to recommend this book to the parents of the next generation and to all of our young patriots who truly care about the direction of our country, the current status of our country, and what it will take to regain our liberties. I firmly believe that our Founders would stand proud and boldly proclaim that this simple, yet profound, work contains the answers America needs to hear.

Shane F. Krauser

Director, American Academy for Constitutional Education

Three facts that every YOUNG American needs to realize...

 1) The United States of America was & is the greatest nation on Earth.

 2) Today, the United States of America is in serious trouble.

 3) You will inherit the USA—and its problems—in just a few short years.

Whoa. Did that get your attention? Hope so.

Now, I don't mean to start this book on a downer.

. . . but hopefully you are intrigued enough to keep reading. As young Americans, it's crucial that you understand and appreciate these three facts. Let me explain:

FACT #1
The United States of America was & is the greatest nation on Earth.

September 17, 1787—Constitutional Convention

"Gentlemen, as we have sat here, discussing and debating this document, I have wondered to myself . . .

"That sun painted on the back of Mr. Washington's chair . . . is it a rising or a setting sun?"

"And what have you decided, Dr. Franklin?"

"Indeed, it is a rising sun."*

*true story[1]

What did Benjamin Franklin mean by "a rising sun?"

On that day, our Founding Fathers signed the Constitution, forming a nation unlike anything the world had ever known. This new government was to be a Republic . . . created by the people, for the people. It protected certain God-given rights, rights that no government could diminish. It secured life, liberty, and the pursuit of happiness. It offered freedom. It was to be a rising sun in a dark world.

These good men, inspired by God, created your nation . . . the United States of America.

TIME OUT!

You've heard this kind of talk before.

You have a basic understanding of our nation's beginnings.

You know about George Washington, Benjamin Franklin, James Madison, and the other Founding Fathers. You respect them and admire what they did. You may not know *all* the particulars of the Constitution ... or *all* the principles behind our nation's founding (not yet, at least ☺) ... but you know enough to realize that what these wise men accomplished was good.

 **But do you realize HOW good?**

How 'bout good enough to change the course of human history!

Ever since it's founding, the United States of America has been a light to all other nations. It has become the model of what the power of freedom can do. The world, by following America's example, has progressed and advanced more in the past 200-plus years than in all the 5,000 years of history previous. Wow! A rising sun indeed!

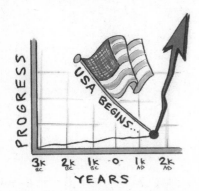 **All thanks to the ideas and principles that were the founding of this nation.**

In other words . . .

You've looked back to THEIR day and sensed the greatness of what our Founding Fathers accomplished: namely, the creation of this God-inspired, one-of-a-kind "experiment" called the United States of America.

BUT . . .

What if these Founding Fathers could see OUR day?

- What if they went **FORWARD** through time and could see the state of our nation today?

- No doubt they would be amazed at the **GROWTH** and **PROGRESS** of their USA "experiment." But what about the direction our nation is **HEADED**?

- How true have we been to the **PRINCIPLES** upon which this nation was founded?

- How true have we been lately to the **CONSTITUTION** that they wrote and signed?

- ## WOULD THEY BE PLEASED OR NOT?

- Hmmmm, I wonder . . .

(cue "going back in time" harp music)

Some time shortly after the signing of the Constitution . . .

Gentlemen, with this machine, we can actually travel forward through time—into the FUTURE! Certainly you are as curious as I am to see the destiny of this American experiment. Well, now we can!

It's history in reverse! Will the people stay true to this nation's founding principles? Will they stay true to the Constitution we just signed?

Will America continue to be a rising sun? These are the questions.

So, how far forward in time shall we go? A few hundred years or so into the future? The 2000s, perhaps?

Here it is!!

The moment of truth!

What will they find?

And after a THOROUGH exploration of the state of our nation, our government, our attitudes about government, our regard for the Constitution, our politics, our values, and so on and so forth, IN MODERN TIMES—here is their reaction . . .

Okay, let's freeze for a moment...

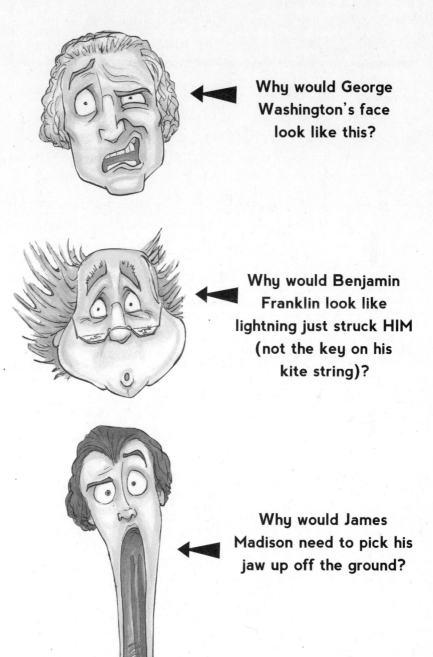

Why would George Washington's face look like this?

Why would Benjamin Franklin look like lightning just struck HIM (not the key on his kite string)?

Why would James Madison need to pick his jaw up off the ground?

FACT #2

Today, the United States of America is in serious trouble.

Along with sensing that the founding of this nation was good, you've probably also sensed that the current state of our nation is **NOT GOOD**.

Something's wrong. You're not sure what it is exactly, but there are too many clues for you to ignore, even as a young person. Clues pointing to the fact that things are not right in this great nation of ours.

You may have overheard your parents talking about certain problems our country faces. You've noticed news headlines. Perhaps you've listened to talk radio hosts or TV personalities going off about how "off track" America is today. You may have heard about *this* crisis or caught tidbits of information about *that* issue. You'd like to understand it all, but you just get more confused.

National Healthcare

GOVERNMENT BAILOUTS

Federal Deficit

The Economy

INFLATION

Illegal Immigration

HOME MORTGAGE CRISIS

Tax Increases

In other words, you're aware that something is wrong today . . . but you don't know what it is.

WHY is our country in serious trouble?

What is the **CORE PROBLEM**?

HOW has our nation gotten "off track" from what the Founding Fathers established?

What does getting "off track" **EVEN MEAN** exactly?

WHAT'S GOING ON?!

And could someone please explain it in a way that WE can understand?

Oh, and let's not forget . . .

YOU will inherit the USA— and its problems—in just a few short years.

Yup, it's true. You won't be "young" forever. You will grow into adults.

Shocking, I know.

This is *your* nation. It's yours to inherit, assume command, take the reins, be given the car keys, and so on.

Because of this fact, I believe you are concerned. You want to be informed. You aren't just shallow-minded kids whose biggest care in the world is what people are posting on your Facebook wall. You think deeper than some adults give you credit for. You want to gain knowledge so that when the time comes, you can DO SOMETHING about this "serious trouble" we are in!

After all, our nation is only as good as its next generation . . . and that is you.

And that, my young friend, is the purpose of this book: to help you appreciate the *wisdom of our nation's origins* and, by contrast, understand the *problems with its current state.*

AND ... we'll have some fun doing it. ☺

And if you're one of those people who's thinking, "Oh, this stuff is **boring**" ... well then, you just haven't really been taught yet! It's anything but boring!

Once you truly grasp what made/makes this nation great, you won't ever be the same. A fire will be ignited in you that won't easily be extinguished. And when enough of you young patriots get that fire burnin' inside you, you will restore this nation back to what made it so great in the first place.

Shall we get started then? Great!

Let's unfreeze our Founding Father's faces and continue with the story.

Perhaps they will shed some light on ...

What was intended for this nation <u>back then</u>

vs.

What is happening in this nation <u>today</u>

I got it! We turn our attention to the
YOUNG people—the rising generation!
We teach *them*!
They are clean slates, ready to learn.
After all, a nation is only as good
as its next generation.

You're right, George!
They're untarnished
by these "modern"
political ideals. If we
teach *them* the principles
that are the foundation
of this nation, they could
change everything.
But how do we
reach them?

Aha, my friends,
I believe I could
be of assistance
in that regard!
My Future
Forecaster has
one more feature
I must show you.

This contraption will allow you to speak with anyone in the world. Simply push this button here, and look into this little circle, and speak. They will see and hear everything you say. This way we will be able to "**S**hare **K**nowledge w/**Y**oung **P**eople **E**verywhere." S-K-Y-P-E. I call it "SKYPE," for short.

And then, if these fine young Americans have questions, they "**C**an **H**ave **A T**urn" asking those questions and their words will appear on this screen. C-H-A-T. I call that "CHAT"-ing, for short.

Well then, what are we waiting for? George? Would you care to go first?

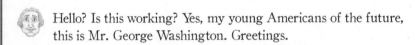 Hello? Is this working? Yes, my young Americans of the future, this is Mr. George Washington. Greetings.

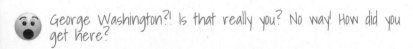 George Washington?! Is that really you? No way! How did you get here?

Uh, yes . . . it's really me. And you can accredit our presence here to Franklin's Fantastic Future Forecaster. As a matter of fact, Benjamin Franklin and James Madison are here with me as well.

 Hello, fellow Americans.

 Yes, greetings.

 LOL. How cool is this!

Yes, LOL to you as well. Anyway, to get straight to the point, my young friends . . . we have seen your day and are very concerned about the state of this nation.

Okay? What do you mean?

In your day, it seems that many people have forgotten or tried to change what the United States of America is all about. We would like to remedy that. We want to teach you what we intended for this country when we wrote and signed the Constitution. We trust that you young people, when given knowledge, can one day return your nation back to the principles on which it was founded.

May we discuss these things with you?

Of course! That would be totally awesome!

Splendid! Let us get started then. And please, feel free to ask questions as we go.

Sounds great! We're all ears!

Imagine that the United States of America is a giant pyramid.

How do you build a pyramid? Well, you start with a large, sturdy foundation and then work up.

When we began this nation, its foundation was . . .

GOD & RELIGION

GOD & RELIGION

"The longer I live, the more convincing Proofs I see of this Truth—That God governs in the Affairs of Men."[2]

-Benjamin Franklin

My young Americans, let it be known that we believed in God. We were dependant on God. We turned to Him for help. Our belief in God was the main reason we settled this land. God & Religion was and is the backbone of this nation. It has always been so, despite what critics in your time might say.

For example, without God's help, there is no way our tiny, inexperienced colonial army could have won the Revolutionary War against the mighty British army. As general of that colonial army, I saw that with my own eyes. God's hand has always been over this land, blessing this nation.[3]

They are retreating sir!

 And I suggested we pray and ask for God's help when we were writing the Constitution. I knew that without Divine help, the separate states would never be able to come to an agreement over that document. We needed to turn to God.[4]

 And He did help us! The signing of the Constitution was indeed a miracle! All of us who were involved in that great event would agree to that.

A belief in God is so important that we cannot emphasize it enough.[5]

GOD & RELIGION

Excuse me, I have a question.

Please, yes . . . feel free to ask at any time.

But there are so many <u>different</u> religions and beliefs about God. People sometimes even fight over religion. Is it okay that everyone in the country doesn't believe exactly the same thing?

 Oh, yes! Certainly. We want people to have the freedom to worship however they choose. We wrote about that in the First Amendment of the Constitution. But these religious differences should never cause contention or arguing. Instead, Americans should be **united** and **strengthened** by the religious beliefs they have in **common**.

For example, what unites **all** the religions is the belief that:

- **There is a God who created and rules the universe**

- **We should worship that God**

- **We should treat others the way we want to be treated (often called "The Golden Rule")**

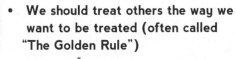

- **After this life, we will be responsible for what we did here on Earth.**[6]

These are the fundamental points in all sound religion, and they are powerful beliefs indeed! They teach us right from wrong! They are the foundation of our society and of our government. They unite us as a people. That's why we wanted these common beliefs taught in our schools.

 Really? Religion was a part of your schools back then?

Of course! Our schools were permitted (encouraged even) to teach the basic religious concepts that were universally accepted by all faiths.[7] For example, just look at what Congress wrote in an ordinance that was passed the very same year the Constitution was signed:

> "Religion, morality, and knowledge being necessary to good government and the happiness of mankind, schools and the means of education shall forever be encouraged"
> (Northwest Ordinance, Article 3).

Side Order of Fries

(Okay, this is where we officially break away from the SKYPE/CHAT dialogue to share a cool little tidbit on the subject.)

In 1831, a young Frenchman named Alexis de Tocqueville came to the United States to study our country. We were so different than any European nation and he wanted to learn what made us tick. De Tocqueville was amazed at what he saw!

GOD & RELIGION

"Upon my arrival in the United States the religious aspect of the country was the first thing that struck my attention" [8]

Sacré bleu!

He goes on to observe that *"each [religious] sect adores [God] in its own peculiar manner, but all sects preach the same moral law in the name of God."* [9]

Sounds like what Benjamin Franklin just mentioned, right? The US citizens of the time were united by the religious beliefs they had in common.

BUT . . . what about religion and politics (since this book is about government)?! Could those two concepts ever work together?? Do they have to be separate? What do you have to say about THAT, Mr. De Tocqueville??

"In France I had almost always seen the spirit of religion and the spirit of freedom marching in opposite directions." [10] **But in America, he says** that *"[religion] contributed powerfully to the establishment of a republic and a democracy in public affairs; and from the beginning, <u>politics and religion contracted an alliance which has never been dissolved.</u>"* [11]

Wow. You mean, back then, <u>basic religious concepts</u> and <u>government</u> COEXISTED . . . TOGETHER . . . IN HARMONY??

"Oui, oui."

(That's "yes" in French. And it's pronounced "we, we," not "ow, ow." ☺).

Yes, my young friend, a belief in God was strongly encouraged in our time! We knew that having a religious people would lead to the next level of our pyramid, which is . . .

VALUES & VIRTUES

"Our Constitution was made only for a <u>moral</u> and <u>religious</u> people. It is wholly inadequate to the government of any other."[12]

-John Adams

When people put God first in their lives, it affects every part of them. They treat others fairly and with respect. They show kindness. They try to follow God's commandments and be good citizens. This leads naturally to the development of **VALUES & VIRTUES**.

They also tend to be happier. I believe God wants me to be happy, and since happiness comes only through living virtuously, I firmly believe God wants me to have values and virtues.[13]

Whaddya mean by "values and virtues"? You mean like "building character"? My parents use that phrase with me all the time. ☺

And well they should!

Values and Virtues are all those good things your parents teach you to do, that you know you <u>should</u> do, that are sometimes <u>hard</u> to do, but you always feel better about yourself when you do them. Simply put, having values is making smart choices and doing what's right. When you make these right choices often enough, they become good habits.

Here are a few Values & Virtues that Americans NEED for this nation to work the way we intended:

Be RESPONSIBLE!

THEN

Be someone people can count on. Do what you're supposed to do, even if it's hard or you don't feel like it. Don't be a "slacker" as you would say. And don't blame other people for your actions. You are in charge of you! Take responsibility for yourself. Know right from wrong . . . and choose the right!

NOW

VIRTUES & VALUES

Be a HARD WORKER!

Learn the value of work. Learn how to work for things that you want and earn them. And while you work for those things, be patient. Don't expect to have everything you want right away. Don't expect to have things you didn't work for and earn. Don't complain about working, but find satisfaction in it. Do a good job and stick to it 'til the job is done.

THEN

NOW

Be GENEROUS!

Think about what other people need. Don't just think about yourself all the time. Look for ways to help others in your home, in your school, in your community, anywhere! Share. Be kind. Serve. Smile. Give of yourself for the benefit of others. Follow the Golden Rule: Do to others what you would want them to do to you.

THEN

NOW

Be HONEST

Tell the truth. Be someone people can trust. Don't lie, steal, or cheat . . . even if you think you won't get caught. Don't take credit for things you didn't do. Be true to yourself. Live honorably.

I cannot tell a lie.

Now I must be HONEST. We're not sure if the story of young George Washington cutting down the cherry tree really happened or not, but surely "telling the truth" was important to him. ☺

THEN

NOW

In short, people WITH strong values work at becoming the very best they can be! They strive for excellence.

HOW HIGH
I CAN FLY?

 These are just a few key values we hope you young people will strive for. There are many more values to learn.

VIRTUES & VALUES

Side Order of Fries

Did you know that Benjamin Franklin wasn't too happy about making the bald eagle our national bird. True story. And guess what his reason was? "(The bald eagle) is a bird of bad moral Character. He does not get his Living honestly."[14]

He then explains how the "lazy" bald eagle waits around for other birds to catch their food and then while that other bird is taking its dinner home to its family, the bald eagle steals that fish for itself.

Yea, I know. For rude, Mr. Bald Eagle! Sorry. Instinct.

See . . . Benjamin Franklin even wanted the character of our national bird to be in harmony with our values and virtues.

So, Mr. Franklin, if not the bald eagle, what bird should we have used?

"The turkey is in comparison a much more respectable bird"
(yes, that's a direct quote).

Okay, I'm kinda glad the other Founding Fathers outvoted Franklin on this one.

As our good friend John Adams said at the beginning of this pyramid level, **"This Constitution was made only for a moral and religious people. It is wholly inadequate to the government of any other."** That means they must have values & virtues for the American experiment to even work.

 But why, Mr. Madison?? Why do people have to have these "Values & Virtues" for America to work right? Shouldn't we just be able to do whatever we want, since it's a "free country"? I don't get it.

That, my young friend, is a profound question. **Why** are these values so essential? And this will be the focus of the rest of our discussion. When we're finished, I think it will all make sense.

 Excuse me, James, but might I give an example that I believe will help them understand **what freedom is** and **how it actually works**. I'll use an activity that I'm familiar with:

"Hello, Mr. Franklin, sir. What are you doing?"

"Hello, young man. Why, I'm flying this kite."

VIRTUES & VALUES

So then, in this example, if the kite represents you and me, what do you suppose the kite *string* represents?

uh . . . probably our Values & Virtues?

Precisely! So many in your time have it backwards. They think that living by values & virtues is too restrictive and keeps you from being free to do whatever you want.

But values & virtues are actually what give us freedom, just as the kite string allowed the kite to fly. In other words, **"Only a virtuous people are capable of freedom."**[15] That's why your parents try so hard to teach you these things.

So, when the citizens of our nation are "capable" of this freedom, because they live by God-given values, it takes us to the next level of our pyramid, which is . . . George? Would you like to continue?

PEOPLE GOVERN THEMSELVES

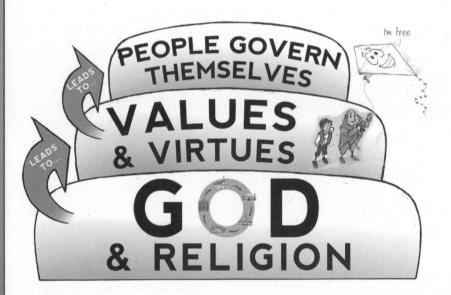

PEOPLE GOVERN
THEMSELVES

"We have staked the future of all of our political institutions upon the capacity of each and all of us to govern ourselves according to the Ten Commandments of God."[16]

-James Madison

When people live virtuous lives, according to positive values, they then have the power to truly **govern themselves.**

 Wait, time out. I'm not sure I understand. Why do values & virtues give people the freedom to "govern themselves"?? Can't anyone be in charge of themselves if they want to. I'm still not getting this "values equals freedom" thing.

That's understandable. Your modern media is constantly filling your head with messages of "Freedom without rules!" "Just do whatever feels good!" "Don't worry about the consequences!" And that is part of the reason our beloved country is struggling so much in your time.

Let me see if I can further explain this idea. Listen carefully. I'll use the four values & virtues we just mentioned . . .

- **Because the people know how to work, they are free to work hard, acquire property, and improve their lives (LIFE).**

- **Because the people are responsible, they are free to be in charge of their own actions (LIBERTY).**

- **Because the people are generous, they are free to share and help others when they choose (LIBERTY).**

- **Because the people are honest, they are free to make good choices and, thus, find happiness through those good choices (THE PURSUIT OF HAPPINESS).**

In short, they are free to govern their lives without anybody controlling them, because they know how to control themselves. They also don't depend on others to do everything for them, because they can take care of themselves. They are free of addictions. They are self-motivated. Various doors of opportunity are opened to them because they know how to work hard, can be trusted, and are responsible.

PEOPLE GOVERN
THEMSELVES

In other words, they can enjoy productive, meaningful lives . . . all because of their values. And that, my young friends, is real freedom. The freedom to succeed.

 Hmmm. Well, when you put it that way . . . ☺ Okay, it makes more sense.

Excellent! Let's continue then . . . Mr. Madison? I believe you are most qualified to teach this next point.

 Thank you, Mr. Washington.

When we founded this nation, we did NOT want a king!

A king has TOO much power. We knew that a king would start to take freedoms away from the people.

And in addition, a king does not have the RIGHT to rule over people. God gives PEOPLE the right to govern THEMSELVES! This is a key point—**the PEOPLE have the power.** As I once said, "The ultimate authority . . . resides in the people alone." It is sometimes called **popular sovereignty.** That is why the first three words of the U.S. Constitution are "We the People."

So, why have a government and a Constitution at all, then? If the People have all the power to "govern themselves," then why do we still need leaders or a government?

A fine question! What *is* the purpose of establishing a government? And your answer is the next step of the pyramid. Mr. Franklin, would you like to explain the purpose of government?

LIMITED GOVERNMENT
protects people's rights

"The powers delegated
by the Constitution to
the federal government are
few and defined."[17]

-James Madison

A government's main purpose is this.
To **PROTECT** those freedoms Mr. Washington just mentioned:

LIFE, LIBERTY, and THE PURSUIT OF HAPPINESS.

These are called **unalienable rights.** That means God (not government) gave each person the right to enjoy these things and nobody has the power to take these rights away. We wrote about them in the Declaration of Independence.

> *"We hold these truths to be self-evident, that all men are created equal, that they are* ***endowed by their Creator with certain unalienable Rights,*** *that among these are Life, Liberty and the pursuit of Happiness. —* ***That to secure these rights, Governments are instituted among Men,*** *deriving their just powers from the consent of the governed."*

Note the part that reads, "That to secure these rights, Governments are instituted among Men."

That means the government's job is simply to **PROTECT THE PEOPLE'S RIGHTS THEY ALREADY HAVE.**

Side Order of Fries

Did you know that the original phrase used by the founding fathers was that all people "are entitled to life, liberty, and PROPERTY?" Being able to own property without the fear of government or someone else taking it from them was one of the most important rights a government could protect!

LIMITED
GOVERNMENT

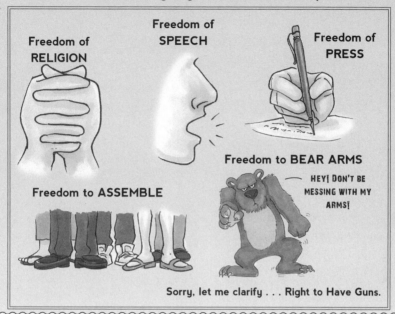

Some other unalienable rights government is sworn to protect are:

Freedom of RELIGION

Freedom of SPEECH

Freedom of PRESS

Freedom to ASSEMBLE

Freedom to BEAR ARMS

HEY! DON'T BE MESSING WITH MY ARMS!

Sorry, let me clarify . . . Right to Have Guns.

Wait a minute . . . That's it? That's the government's only real job? To "protect our rights"?

Basically, yes. The government's power is LIMITED to that. Let me explain why.

Did you catch that last part of the Declaration of Independence clip?

" . . . deriving their just powers from the consent of the governed."

That means that since governments are created by the people, then government can only have powers that . . .

1) the people themselves have
AND
2) that the people choose to give to the government

 Excuse me, Mr. Franklin, sir? This is getting kinda confusing again . . . Can you give us another example, maybe?

Of course! We really need you to understand this idea . . .

GOOD GOV PRODUCTIONS

PRESENTS . . .

THE GOOD, THE BAD, AND A BUNCH OF COWS

Mooo ooo ooooo.
Waah. waah. waaaah.

✷ SCENE 1 ✷

This is Rich and his family. They are ranchers who lived back in what you call the Old West.

✷ SCENE 2 ✷

This is Bandit Bob and his posse. They like to sneak onto Rancher Rich's land and steal his cows.

✷ SCENE 3 ✷

These are other families in the area. They are having the same problem with Bandit Bob stealing their cows.

LIMITED
GOVERNMENT

SCENE 4

One day, all
these families
get together and
elect Shane to be
their sheriff.

SCENE 5

They give Sheriff
Shane the POWER to
protect their RIGHT
to own PROPERTY
(their cows).

SCENE 6

Sheriff Shane
puts an end to
Bandit Bob's cow
stealing days.

The End

Now, at what point in the story did the people "create government"?

 Umm, maybe when they made that guy sheriff?

Correct. And what power did they give the sheriff?

The power to stop Bandit Bob from stealing their cows.

So, let me ask two questions: First, did the people have the right to protect their own cows (their property) from being stolen?

Of course! Bandit Bob can't just take those people's cows like that. They don't belong to him.

Okay. And, second, did the people willingly give that power (to protect their cows) to the sheriff?

Yes.

Excellent. Then their government (Sheriff Shane) passed the two-part test! He was doing what government was allowed to do: Use power that . . .

1) the people themselves already have
AND
2) that the people choose to give to the government

In other words, government can't just do whatever it wants. That's what we mean by LIMITED government. Does that make sense?

 Totally. Thanks!

LIMITED
GOVERNMENT

When the people have values & virtues . . .

they elect government leaders who have values & virtues.

VALUES & VIRTUES

These good men and women serve as their leaders for a time. Their job is to **REP**RESENT the people they are assigned over (that's where we get the word **REP**UBLIC). They listen to the needs of the people to try to serve them better. They protect their rights. Because these leaders are virtuous people, they won't start doing things that go beyond their right, as a government, to do.

Governments help **protect us,**

educate us,   **settle disputes,**   **make needed laws,**

and do a few other things . . .

all to help the people enjoy their rights.

They are not supposed to be involved in every little part of your life!

Okay, when you say "government" . . . aren't there like different kinds of government? Like different levels?

Yes, thank you for bringing that up.

The smallest and closest government to you is your . . .

 **FAMILY**

My family?! That's a "government"?

Certainly! Your parents provide structure, rules, leadership, protection, education—all in a spirit of love. That's a government . . . the best kind of government, really.

Next comes your **CITY/TOWN** government. Maybe you've been to a city council meeting before.

Then comes your **COUNTY** government.

Then the **STATE** government.

And last is the **FEDERAL** government that is over the entire country.

LIMITED
GOVERNMENT

Okay, got it!

 Good. Now, my young Americans, please remember this:

THE MORE LOCAL THE GOVERNMENT, THE BETTER IT IS AT KNOWING THE NEEDS OF ITS PEOPLE!

For example:
Who knows better what you need at home?

| Your parents who love you | –OR– | Some person 1,000 miles away who doesn't know you? |

Who knows better what you need at school?

| Your teacher/ principal | –OR– | Some person 1,000 miles away who works in an office? |

Who knows better what your town needs?

| Your town council | –OR– | Some person 1,000 miles away who doesn't even know your town exists? |

Who knows better what your state needs?

Your State Government –OR– some person who . . .

LOL, we get the point. Local is good! ☺

Yes, local IS good. Local governments do a better job because they are more in touch with the needs of the people they represent. Plus, the more decisions are made at a LOCAL level, the more people feel a responsibility for governing themselves (which is a good thing).

That is why we wanted the order of influence of the different types of government to go like this. It starts at the bottom and works up:

But wait a minute! I thought the Federal government . . . you know, like the President, and Congress, and those people . . . should be the BIGGEST, with the MOST power. Why's it so tiny and only at the tippy-top? I don't get it.

Because we designed it that way! It all goes back to the idea of **limited** government.

The Federal government was to be **limited** to only a **few** powers—such as the military (defending our nation), foreign relations (dealing with other countries), and interstate commerce (business between the states).

Okay. Here are your powers. Now, don't go asking for more.

ALL other powers not mentioned in the Constitution are given to the states and local governments. We wrote that specifically into the **Tenth Amendment.**

LIMITED
GOVERNMENT

Really?

Yes. And to *keep* the Federal Government's power **limited,** we divided it into **three** different branches

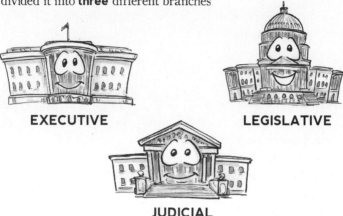

EXECUTIVE **LEGISLATIVE**

JUDICIAL

But how does that limit their power? Doesn't that make them three times more powerful?

Actually, it does just the opposite. The three branches of federal Government **check** on each other and **balance** each other out, keeping any one branch from getting too powerful. It's called checks and balances.

For example, the Executive branch (the President) can't just make laws without the consent of the Legislative branch (Congress). While at the same time, the President has the power to veto (say "no" to) bills that are passed by Congress. And the Judicial branch checks these laws and decides whether they are constitutional (agree with the Constitution) or not.

It's all in the Constitution.

Quick question about the Constitution: I know it's a good thing. I don't really understand it all. Why does everyone make such a big deal about the Constitution again?

 James, we consider you to be the Father of the Constitution. Why don't you keep explaining?

 The Constitution is the written instruction sheet on how to govern this blessed nation.

We know God inspired us when we wrote it. It gives the government structure and limits. Different leaders come and go, but the Constitution stays the same. It's constant! Government leaders promise to always uphold and follow the Constitution. If a leader gets an idea to do something that is not allowed in the Constitution, he or she can't do it. They are bound by the Constitution.

That is why every US President makes this pledge before they take office:

 "I do solemnly swear (or affirm) that I will faithfully execute the Office of President of the United States, and will to the best of my Ability, preserve, protect and defend the Constitution of the United States."

 ## Side Order of Curly Fries

The only way to add to the Constitution is to make an official amendment. This is a long process that requires a lot of support from congress. It's not easy to do . . . which is good. Because then leaders can't just casually add to the Constitution willy-nilly . . . whenever they feel like it.

Did I just say willy-nilly? ☺

LIMITED
GOVERNMENT

Let me ask *you* a question now.

Imagine for a moment that our nation did NOT have the Constitution. *Without* the Constitution defining and limiting the government's power, what would stop the government from doing whatever it wanted?

 Nothing, I guess. Hmmmm, I see your point. That would be kinda scary to give them that much power.

Why?

Because governments are run by people, and people do crazy things when they get too much power. We learned all about that in world history. Most of the kings in history were pretty much jerks. They didn't seem to care about the people they ruled over. They just wanted more land and more power.

 Very sad, but very true. That is why the people of this nation, who love the Constitution, don't WANT the government to have all that power. They want a . . .

LIMITED GOVERNMENT to Protect their Rights . . .

So they can be free to **GOVERN THEMSELVES** . . .

Because they have **VALUES & VIRTUES** . . .

Based on their **RELIGION** and faith in **GOD**.

See, it all goes back to the pyramid. Quite simple, really.

LIMITED
GOVERNMENT

Yeah... I think I get it. It makes sense. Cool!

This is what we intended for the United States of America when we signed the Constitution. This is what it means to be an American: We trust in God and put Him first.

. . . one nation, <u>under God,</u> indivisible, with liberty and justice for all.

We live moral, virtuous lives. We take responsibility for governing ourselves. We honor the family unit. We cherish our God-given rights and establish governments to protect those rights.

Following this pyramid is what has made this nation great. It's what makes us unique. And it's what gives this nation strength and stability. Always remember that and don't let anyone tell you otherwise.

Okay.

Now, before we go to part two of this lesson, I believe a 30-minute recess is in order. Agreed?

Yes! I gotta text my friends to make sure they are watching this also. This is good stuff. See ya in 30.

Side Order of Breadsticks

(to go with our pizza)

At the close of the Constitutional Convention in 1787, Americans were very interested in knowing what kind of government the state delegates had come up with. After all, they had met in private for four months! Americans were anxious to hear what they decided. As they were leaving the convention, a certain lady approached Benjamin Franklin . . .

"Well, Doctor, what have we got, a republic or a monarchy?"

"A republic . . . IF you can keep it."[18]

Why would the wise Benjamin Franklin add the "if you can keep it" part? What was his point? Think about that as we go on to the SECOND part of our Founding Father SKYPE/CHAT session.

(30 minutes later)

 My young Americans, are you ready to continue?

 Yup! This is great! Hey, are those pizza boxes behind you?

Ahhemm. Anyway, as we were saying . . .

In the beginning, the structure of the United States of America was based on the pyramid we have just discussed. When things are in their proper place and size, it is very strong and stable.

However, after observing things in **YOUR** day, we fear the pyramid structure of this nation is significantly **DIFFERENT**.

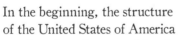

It starts with a much smaller, much weaker base . . .

LACK OF GOD & RELIGION

"We have grown in numbers, wealth and power as no other nation has ever grown. But we have forgotten God."[19]

-Abraham Lincoln

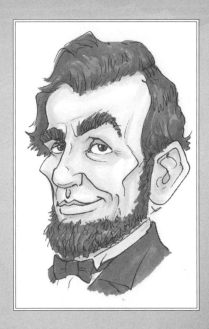

Overall, it seems that God & Religion are playing a much smaller role in America than they did in our day.

Although there are still many religious Americans, there are a great many who are not. They have forgotten God. They do not feel a dependence on Him like we did. God & Religion are not high priorities in their everyday lives. They are distracted by other things. In your day, we see religion portrayed as being "old-fashioned" and "out of touch" with modern times. Sometimes your modern media downright mocks people of faith.

We could say quite a bit more about the decline of God & Religion in your time, but suffice it to say that the influence of God & Religion in the United States, as a whole, has been on a steady decline for a number of years.

 Yes, indeed. And we've seen that some people even want to remove God *completely* from this Nation. They want to . . .

Remove God from your money

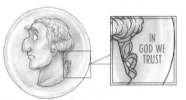

Remove God from the Pledge of Allegiance

. . . one nation, under **the sky,** indivisible . . .

Keep God from being talked about in school

Then, because of my faith in God, I decided to . . .

Next report please.

Basically, keep God from being mentioned in ANY public place

>BLEEP< bless America

LACK OF RELIGION & GOD

I know, I know—I've seen that in MY school! We totally can't talk about God there. But if you guys could pray in public and talk about God in your schools and all that . . . why can't we do it now? What happened??

Let me see if I can explain . . .

All throughout history, people have not had the freedom to worship however they choose. Whatever the king said about religion, the people had to follow. The king's religion was part of the government and it controlled the people's lives.

We did not want that for America. We designed the Constitution to allow people the freedom to worship God however they wanted, without the government getting in the way.

In other words, **freedom of religion was to be protected from the government interfering.**

HOWEVER . . . we *also* knew that religion in general has a good influence over the government because it keeps our leaders virtuous (Remember: God & Religion leads to Values & Virtues). So, the basic beliefs that all religions have in common (that we discussed in the first pyramid) were encouraged!

In other words, government was NOT to be protected from religious freedom, but influenced BY religious freedom.

In your day, some people have completely changed what we meant. They say there is a wall that COMPLETELY separates religion and government (which includes your school). These people say you can't mention God at all because you might offend someone who does not believe in God. Thus, they take away your religious freedom . . . your right TO talk about God.

 And, Benjamin, don't forget—when government is not being influenced by basic religion, it is also not being influenced by religion's Values & Virtues and is more likely to become corrupt.

I'm not sure I understand.

How about another example then:

 = **Religious Freedom**   = **Government**

1) Before our nation was born, **governments** (usually a king) feared **religious freedom** (fire) because it threatened their power.

 2) They could extinguish the fire easily because it had no protection.

3) The fire died and it was cold and dark.

Then came the United States of America.

 = **The First Amendment, US Constitution**

4) **The First Amendment** (the pot belly stove) protects **religious freedom** (the fire) from being extinguished easily by the **government** (the man). And it protects the Man from being taken over by an out of control fire.

LACK OF
RELIGION & GOD

BUT REMEMBER!
The man and the fire are only separated by thin iron walls and a glass door!

5) **Government** (the man) can still feel all the positive effects of **religious freedom** (the fire), like heat, light, and overall "coziness" (values & virtues that religion supports). And the government is free to help religious freedom thrive (put more logs on the fire), which benefits everyone.

Ahhhh.

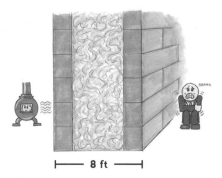

|← 8 ft →|

6) In *your* day, the government is trying to build between him and religious freedom a "wall of separation" that is made of **solid stone** and is **eight feet thick**! It keeps out all the values and virtues (the heat and light) that religious freedom gives off. Thus, the fire doesn't do him much good, does it?

Nope. He's still pretty cold and in the dark. Okay, that makes sense. But can't you still have values & virtues without God and religion?

Well, in our analogy, could the man enjoy heat and light without the fire?

Uh . . . I guess not.

Always remember:
We cannot get rid of God and religious principles and expect the people to stay strong in their values.

In other words, a **Lack of God & Religion** leads to a . . .

LACK OF VALUES & VIRTUES

LACK OF
VIRTUES & VALUES

"If we lose these virtues or pursue the opposite of them, then the great cause that we know as America will be betrayed, dishonored, and finally destroyed."[20]

-James Madison

If we, as a nation, lack values & virtues, then we are in a terrible situation indeed! I once said, **"To suppose that any form of government will secure liberty or happiness without any virtue in the people, is a [false] idea."** [21] Here's why:

When people don't learn how to be **RESPONSIBLE**, they become . . .

<u>IRRESPONSIBLE</u>. They don't take responsibility for their actions. They cannot be depended on to do what's right. They don't do their duties. They break rules. And they blame other people for their problems.

When people don't learn how to **WORK HARD**, they become . . .

<u>LAZY</u>. They don't want to work, but only want to be taken care of. They lack motivation. They want everything to be done for them. And they want to be given things right away. They think they "deserve" lots of privileges, even if they didn't earn them.

When people don't learn how to be **GENEROUS**, they become . . .

<u>SELF-CENTERED</u>. They don't share. They don't serve. They don't care about helping other people. Other people don't matter. They think only about themselves. They only care about what makes them feel good.

LACK OF
VIRTUES & VALUES

When people don't learn how to be **HONEST**, they become . . .

DISHONEST. They don't care about telling the truth. They try to get away with lying and cheating, whether it's at school, at work, or at home. They will do anything, even if it's wrong, as long as it makes life better for them.

In short, people WITHOUT strong values don't work toward becoming anything.

HOW LOW CAN I GO?

So, what happens to them???

Well, let's use the kite string example again to see the result of living WITHOUT values and virtues:

Crash an' burn! Ha! ☺ By the way, I was just wondering . . . . why are people lacking values & virtues NOW? What's so different about our day than back in your day?

LACK OF
VIRTUES & VALUES

Well, along with there being less God & Religion, you also have more **DISTRACTIONS** in your day. You have more free time to do things that might be "fun," but they aren't building your values. You have many inventions (TV, movies, video games, Internet, i-everything) that are amazing—but too often they are filling your heads with ideas that aren't based on Values & Virtues.

 That's true, Benjamin. And, like I said before, the best place to learn these values is at home, in your **FAMILIES.** Forgive me for saying, but in your time, family units (overall) are not as strong as they were in our day. There is less and less teaching happening at home. Families need to play a stronger role in your lives. Will you remind your parents of that, please?

Sure.

 SO, back to your first question, my young Americans—what happens to people who don't have strong values & virtues? Think about the kite.

Well, like I said . . . they crash an' burn. They thought the string was too restricting.

Yes? So, what have they lost?

Uh . . . they've lost . . . lost . . . wait! I got it! They've lost their FREEDOM!! The freedom to FLY!

Exactly! Remember what I said, "Only a virtuous people are capable of freedom." Without values and virtues, people are no longer free to govern themselves.

John Adams, another great patriot of the day, said it this way:

> "Liberty can no more exist without virtue . . . than the body can live without the soul."[22]

Which leads us to the next step in our pyramid . . .

PEOPLE NEED TO BE "GOVERNED"

PEOPLE NEED TO
BE GOVERNED

This new government could "end in despotism, as other forms have done before, when the people have become so corrupted as to need despotic government, being incapable of any other."[23]

(*Despotic* means it has complete power and control.)

-Benjamin Franklin

People who are **irresponsible, lazy, self-centered,** and/or **dishonest** (in other words, lacking values & virtues) need to be governed in **two ways**:

They need to be
CONTROLLED

&

They need to be
TAKEN CARE OF

Allow me to explain this in a way that you, as young people, can relate to. Think about life at your home:

Need to be CONTROLLED—Kids who break rules, don't do their duties, and are dishonest have privileges taken away. They can't be trusted. They get in trouble. They need to have more controls put on them to keep them in line. If they can't make good choices for themselves, then parents have to make choices for them. They have to "face the consequences" of their bad decisions . . . which usually means getting grounded more often.

Aaahhh!

And thus, they have LESS & LESS FREEDOM to make their own choices. Instead, they need to be CONTROLLED.

Need to be TAKEN CARE OF— Kids who are lazy and irresponsible don't do things for themselves. They expect everyone else to do things for them. "Mom will pick up after me, Dad will make sure I get up on time, my sister will do my job if I don't, my study group will do the work for me, and my teacher will give me an 'A' because I'm just so darn cute." These lazy thoughts become lazy habits, leading to people who never really learn how to work for something or achieve high goals.

And thus, they have LESS & LESS FREEDOM to succeed in life. Instead, they need to be TAKEN CARE OF.

Now, what?

PEOPLE NEED TO
BE GOVERNED

Yeah, that all sounds kinda familiar. LOL. But that's just with us and our parents at home! What does that have to do with our nation and our government?

It works the same way! The need to be controlled or taken care of applies to anyone who lacks the values & virtues we've been talking about . . . even adults. Except with adults, instead of their parents controlling or taking care of them, it becomes the government's job.

 Very true, George. Now, in the first pyramid, we talked about unalienable rights, remember?

Yeah, those are rights God has given us that no one can take away.

Correct. And the government's job was to . . . what?

Protect those rights.

Correct again.

In this new pyramid, the people (now lacking in values & virtues) still want government to protect their rights, but they have a new notion of what their so-called "rights" are.

Let's see if this next example helps you understand these new "rights" the people feel entitled to:

 One day, you decide you want to play on your school's basketball team. To do that, you have to try out and see if you "make the team," correct?

Right. By the way . . . how do you know about basketball and Internet and all this other modern stuff? How much of our day have you seen?

Plenty. But that's beside the point. (☺wink)

Now, say there are 25 kids who try out . . . but the coach is only taking 12 players. Which of those 25 kids are going to make the team?

The 12 kids who are the best.

And how did they become "the best," as you say?

They had to work at it! They probably practiced harder than the others kids and got good.

But is that fair to the other 13 kids?

Shouldn't everyone who tried out get to be <u>on</u> the team? Doesn't everybody <u>deserve</u> a spot? Isn't it their <u>right</u> to be on the team?

PEOPLE NEED TO
BE GOVERNED

No. That's not how it works. Everybody had the same chance to try out. They could all go for it. Maybe if one of those 13 kids practiced a little harder, he could have made the team instead.

Exactly! Everyone had the same right to try out for the team. The coach couldn't keep you from trying out because he thought you didn't "look like a basketball player" or because he thought your nose was too big or because he didn't like your grandpa.

**There was no guarantee you would make the team . . .
but all were welcome to try!**

This is a perfect example of how a **LIMITED GOVERNMENT** protects our rights. In this country, each person has the same right to improve their **LIFE**, to have **LIBERTY** based on their own choices, and to **PURSUE HAPPINESS** (note the word "pursue" not "have." Your right is to *go after* happiness, not to *be* happy).

In other words, there is no guarantee you'll have all the things you want, but you are free to "go for it" as you say. It is what enables every citizen to work hard and make something of their lives— regardless of where you are born, what race you are, how poor you are, and so on.

Some call it **"The American Dream."**

(And, unlike trying out for the basketball team, there is no limit to the number of people allowed to make the "American Dream" team. Everyone is free to succeed (or fail) equal to the level of effort they put in).

HOWEVER, people who lack values & virtues don't see it that way. They think it is their "right" to be on the team (not just to try out). So, they will whine to the coach about it.

And if the coach doesn't put them on the team, they will go to the principal and complain that they "deserve" to be on the team and that the coach treated them unfairly.

 But that's dumb! They probably just weren't good enough. Or maybe they didn't prepare enough for the tryouts.

What if that kid who didn't make the team was you?

Well, then . . . then I'd just work harder & try out next year.

Ah, my young friends, it sounds like you have the values of Being Responsible for your actions and of Being a Hard Worker. I compliment you on that.

Side Order of __Free__ Fries

Dude! There's this terrible disease going around, have you heard? It's awful! And it is like . . . everywhere! It totally destroys people and they don't even know it. AND it's WAY contagious! Guys, girls, young people, old people, it doesn't matter . . . ANYONE could have it! YOU could have it! Scary, I know. ☹ It has reached epidemic proportions! Some believe it to be the root cause for the decline of our entire nation—it's THAT widespread and THAT dangerous! ☹

Do you wanna know what it is?? Are you sure??? Okay, it's called . . .

PEOPLE NEED TO
BE GOVERNED

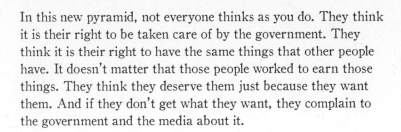

(cue scary music) **THE ENTITLEMENT DISEASE!!!**

(If you're not sure what that word means, ask your parents . . . they'll give you an earful, I'm sure. ☺)

AND . . . there's only one cure. A healthy dose of V&V. Values & Virtues, my friend. It's all about Values & Virtues.

In this new pyramid, not everyone thinks as you do. They think it is their right to be taken care of by the government. They think it is their right to have the same things that other people have. It doesn't matter that those people worked to earn those things. They think they deserve them just because they want them. And if they don't get what they want, they complain to the government and the media about it.

Maximum reward for minimal effort. That is their desire.

But that's messed up. Those aren't their rights. Why do they think like that? Wait a minute . . . I know. Because then they don't have to work for things. They can just do whatever they want, be irresponsible and lazy, and still get all the things they want.

Well put! Maybe we'll just let you teach us now. ☺

 Yeah right. ☺ Sheesh . . . I'm starting to sound like my parents. LOL

I want you to memorize this phrase. Say it five times:

"Government protects your right to TRY, it doesn't provide an EQUAL SUPPLY"

Government protects your right to TRY, it doesn't provide an EQUAL SUPPLY x5 ☺

So, what comes next??

Now we get to the big scary part of the pyramid . . .

BIG GOVERNMENT
takes over!
(Hey, let's hear that girl shriek again! It fits.)

BIG GOVERNMENT

"The natural progress of things is for liberty to yield, and government to gain ground."[24]

-Thomas Jefferson

When the people of this nation start thinking like this—that they are entitled to everything—then the government becomes a whole lot **LARGER**. It takes on a lot more **POWER** as it tries to control and take care of everyone.

And where does government become the largest? At the top.

THE FEDERAL GOVERNMENT.

It stops being a <u>limited</u> government and becomes an <u>unlimited</u> government, taking on more and more mass, squishing the more local governments under its out-of-control weight gain.

 Hold on . . . I just thought of something. What if the government <u>could</u> take care of everyone? Ya know, help everyone out so there's no more poor people and everyone is happy. That doesn't sound so bad to me. Can't the government do that?

smile In your time, artists have created a fictional character named **SUPERMAN**, yes?

Yeah! He's a comic book super hero. He, like, does . . . everything! He flies, is super strong, is super fast, and has super-human powers. And he's always trying to protect people. Yeah, nobody messes with Superman.

Yes, that's the gentleman. We fear that many Americans in your day want the government to be **SUPERMAN**. They think the government has "super powers" to fix all their problems and make everything all right.

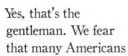
BIG GOVERNMENT

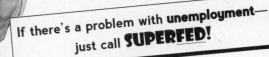

If there's a problem with **unemployment**— just call **SUPERFED!**

If there's a problem with **people being poor**— just call **SUPERFED!**

If there's a problem with the **economy**— just call **SUPERFED!**

If there's a problem with a large company going **bankrupt**— just call **SUPERFED!**

If there's a problem with **health care**— just call **SUPERFED!**

If there's a problem with the **public education**— just call **SUPERFED!**

If there's a problem with **illegal immigration**— just call . . . call . . . uh, **SUPERFED!** Where'd you go?

SUPERFED will save the day! He will solve any and every problem! He can do no wrong! We don't need to worry, **SUPERFED** will take care of us!

However, there is only one big problem with this idea:

What's that?

No one here but mild-mannered Clark Kent.

THE GOVERNMENT IS <u>NOT</u> SUPERMAN!!

FANTASY → REALITY

 Oh.

 Indeed, Dr. Franklin. The government can NOT solve every problem. The government does NOT have super powers to fix everything. The government can NOT rescue everyone and take care of all their needs. The government is NOT run by perfect people who can do no wrong. Political leaders can be incompetent, irresponsible, self-centered, and even dishonest at times.

Side Order of Fries

Okay, you are probably too young to remember this . . . but do you remember **He-Man**? He was kinda like Superman, but with even bigger muscles, no shirt, and a <u>real bad haircut</u>!

There used to be a He-Man cartoon where at some point in each episode, Adam (He-Man's mild-mannered alter ego) lifted his sword and bellowed out "By the Power of Gray Skull . . . **I HAVE THE POWWWEEERRR!!!**" And lightning shot out of his sword, and the music swelled (as did his pecs and biceps), and all of the sudden,

BIG GOVERNMENT

he . . . was . . . HE-MAN! Okay, it was like WAY too cool for a young eight-year-old mind to fathom. ▶

Now, besides whooping up on Skeletor and saving the Universe, Adam/He-Man (much like Clark Kent/Superman) did something else that was truly super amazing:

He didn't fall victim to the corrupting, addictive side of "having the power."

Politicians, on the other hand, are very susceptible to the negative effects of "having the power." Instead of maintaining their values and acting as a servant of the people, they can become corrupt. They can become arrogant, thinking they are better than the people they have been elected to serve. They start focusing on themselves and their careers without thinking about those they represent. They can become addicted to their power and will do everything possible to enlarge themselves and stay in power.

Our wise Founding Fathers understood this fully. They did not even trust themselves to be in a position of absolute power or to be in power for too long.

For example: when the American people began to revere General George Washington as an almost super-human leader—treating him like a king, wanting him to continue being their president beyond his two terms (eight years)—that's when this humble man knew it was time to step down.

So, what keeps our government leaders from abusing their power?

The limits set forth in the Constitution.

At least, that's what the Founding Fathers intended.

So, what happens next??

Well, the people elect leaders who make promises to fix every problem. "Everything will be 'taken care of' if you just elect me," they say. The people want to be "taken care of." They think it's their "right" to be taken care of.

Then the newly elected leader tries to solve all the problems. Not with superpowers, but with (drum roll please) . . . **GOVERNMENT PROGRAMS**! They create more and more government programs to deal with each issue.

Do these programs work?

Some of them help in the short term, but many of these programs don't work very well and are not necessary. Once they are created, they are almost impossible to get rid of. So the programs keep adding up, continually increasing the size of government.

Oh, and these government programs are not free . . . they cost lots and lots of money. How do you suppose the government pays for these programs?

um . . . ask Lois Lane for money?? Jk. I don't know.

BIG GOVERNMENT

Well, they are paid for in **three ways**:

 1) **HIGHER TAXES.** You give more and more of your hard-earned money to the government. *BAD IDEA!*

2) **MAKE MORE MONEY.** The government simply prints off more money, making your money less valuable. It's called Inflation. *BAD IDEA!*

3) **BORROW.** The government borrows money—much of it coming from other countries. The amount of money we owe these people (plus interest) is called the National Debt. *REALLY BAD IDEA!*

So, how much money do we owe in this National Debt?

Well, let's just say it's more money than you can possibly imagine.

 ☹ Oh.

 ☹ Oh, indeed! And, for you young people, here's what is especially bad about America borrowing all this money: **Guess who inherits that debt in the future?**

Good luck!

NATIONAL DEBT

Uh-oh. Let me guess. We do?? You mean we have to pay back the money that we didn't even borrow? The older people are giving us their debt?? That's so not fair! Why does the government keep borrowing and spending money that it doesn't have?

 I wish I knew, my young Americans. Perhaps if people **treat** the government like its Superman, then government leaders start **thinking** they are Superman. They start thinking they can do the impossible. Like making the National Debt magically disappear while they keep spending more money.

When I was president, I continually urged the government to pay off its debts. National debt puts the next generation (you) in a terrible situation.[25] Very Irresponsible, indeed.

Yes, and it gets worse. In trying to be Superman, the federal government **ignores the limits the Constitution gave it**. It takes more and more power from the state and local governments. It wastes huge amounts of money and manpower, meddling in state and local issues that it has no right meddling in. It takes more and more POWER from the American People. It becomes more controlling.

And in its attempts to control and take care of everyone, federal governments even start **taking away the people's God-given rights**.

Do you remember what the **Tenth Amendment** says?

*"The powers not delegated to the United States by the Constitution, nor prohibited by it **to the states**, are reserved to the States respectively, or **to the people**."*

In other words, if the Constitution doesn't specifically mention that the federal government CAN do something, then it is always the responsibility of the smaller governments (or the people).

BIG GOVERNMENT

Side Order of Frog Legs

Right about now you might be asking:

"Dude, how did the federal government get to be so big and lame anyway? Was it all at once or like a gradual thing?"

Good question.

BOILING FROG SYNDROME
(Have you ever heard of it?)

It's said that if you attempt to cook frogs by putting them in a pot of boiling water, they will feel the scalding water and jump right out.

However, if you put those same frogs in a pot of cool water and slowly heat it, they will get used to the slight temperature increase and stay put.

Until, eventually, the water reaches a boiling level and the hot tub party is over (and your scrumptious dinner has just begun! Yum! ☺).

The same idea applies to our government.

The federal government did not just wake up one day and decide to take on all this power. It did not become as **HUGE** as it is today overnight. Americans would not have allowed that. Rather, over the past one hundred years or so, the federal government has been gradually taking on more and more power, one small step at a time. It's been a slow, steady process.

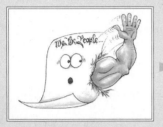

Here a little,   there a little.

And with each small increase in the government's power, Americans would slowly get used to it.

James Madison explained it well when he said, "I believe there are more instances of the abridgment of the freedom of the people by gradual and silent encroachments of those in power, than by violent and sudden usurpations."[26]

What that means is
BOILING FROG SYNDROME

Until today, the Constitution looks something like this. ▶

Of course, leaders often have good intentions when they do something that increases the size of government. Everyone may think it's a great idea. But whether it is a "good idea" is not the issue. What matters is whether what they're trying to do agrees with the guidelines and limits found in the Constitution. Period. End of story.

BIG GOVERNMENT

Wow. That's heavy stuff. Okay, I understand how government can take away power from the people and the local governments. But how does government take away people's God-given rights? Is that even possible?

Well, here's one example. Let's go back to the Sheriff Shane story to explain:

BAD GOV PRODUCTIONS

PRESENTS . . .

THE GOOD, THE BAD, AND A BUNCH OF COWS 2

(Just when you thought it
was safe to own cows again)

★ SCENE 1 ★

Since getting rid
of the Bandit
Bob problem,
everyone
now loves
Sheriff Shane.

THE SHERIFF
IN

MILK

★ SCENE 2 ★

They decide
to keep him as
Sheriff because
he "protects
their rights."

SCENE 3

One day, a sickness hits Unlucky Earl's cows and they all die.

SCENE 4

Sheriff Shane sees this and decides that it's his job to "save the day."

SCENE 5

He goes to Rancher Rich's ranch, flashes his sheriff's badge, takes 20 of Rich's cows, and gives them to Unlucky Earl. Hey, Rich had more cows than he needed anyway. Now everyone is happy, right?

BIG GOVERNMENT

✳ SCENE 6 ✳

Lazy Larry, who only has one cow (because it's too much work to earn the money to buy more cows), sees this and decides THAT would be an easy way to get more cows.

✳ SCENE 7 ✳

Lazy Larry tells Sheriff Shane his sob story about how difficult his life is.

✳ SCENE 8 ✳

Sheriff Shane goes to Wealthy Wayne's ranch, flashes his sheriff's badge, takes 20 of his cows, and gives them to Lazy Larry. Hey, Wayne had more cows than he needed anyway. Now everyone is equal.

Wait a minute, Mr. Franklin! Time out! Stop the story. This is stupid. Sheriff Shane can't do that!

Why not?

Because he can't just take people's cows and give them to anybody he thinks needs them.

Why not? He's the Sheriff. He wants to help Lazy Larry. Isn't that a good thing?

I know, but . . . but . . . he just can't do that!!

I know it **FEELS** wrong to you, but can you tell me **WHY**? Think back on the first pyramid, on how the Sheriff Shane story began. Where did Shane's power come from?

The people. His job was to protect their cows from being stolen. That was the people's God-given right, you said, "to protect their property." And it's their right to simply "own" their property.

Precisely! So, is it a God-given right for you to take someone's property and give it to someone else . . . even if you have good intentions? Of course not! So, if you can't do it, does that mean the Sheriff Shane (the government) can do it?

No! Like you said, rights are God-given, not government given.

Correct. In this example, Rancher Rick and Wealthy Wayne just had their rights **"ARRESTED"** (instead of "protected") by Sheriff Shane.

Sorry.
Instinct.

BIG GOVERNMENT

Remember, government can only have the rights that

1) the people themselves have . . .

AND that 2) the people give to the government.

It doesn't have "superpowers" to do whatever it thinks is good, just because it's the government. <u>The powers are with other people.</u>

Thomas Jefferson explained the role of government when he said,

> **"[A] wise and frugal Government, which shall restrain men from injuring one another, which shall leave them <u>otherwise free to regulate their own pursuits of industry and improvement,</u> and shall not take from the mouth of labor the bread it has earned. This is the sum of good government."**[27]

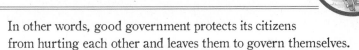

In other words, good government protects its citizens from hurting each other and leaves them to govern themselves.

Man, that just sounds too simple.

Yes, it sounds too simple to you because all you have seen in your lifetime is the **HUGE**, unlimited government we've been talking about. But in **OUR** perspective, Mr. Jefferson's view is right on.

I was just thinking. If I was a rancher and heard about unlucky Earl and all of his cows dying, I would probably just give him some of my cows. Ya know, to help him out and be generous. Wait a minute. Generous. That's one of the values & virtues.

It is, indeed! Now do you see why, as my friend John Adams said, **"This Constitution was made only for a moral and religious people."** When the people are "a moral and religious people" (in other words, have values & virtues), they help each other because they WANT to . . . not because the government makes them.

There are a lot of problems out there and a lot of people do need help. But it is the role of the people, in a spirit of charity and generosity, to assist each other—as individuals, as families, through groups and organizations, through their churches, and so on. It is NOT the government's responsibility or even its right.

Cool. I get it. But how is the government taking people's cows and giving them to other people today?

 (chuckle) The cows represent the people's wealth, their money.

For example: Let's say worked really hard and earned a lot of money one year. It's your money, your property. What if the government told you that when you paid taxes that year, you had to give HALF of that money to them?

You had a good year. Now give me half.

B-b-b-but . . .

 That's lame! To do what with?? Pay for all their government programs?

Then let's say that somebody else earned very little money that year, and the government said they only had to pay 1/10 of that money in taxes.

What?? That's not fair!

And then let's say somebody ELSE didn't work at all that year and just waited for the government to give them money and "take care" of them. Guess who's money they get?

 My tax money?!? Dude, this is making me mad.

Thanks Superfed!

BIG GOVERNMENT

Yes, it's called the Wealth Redistribution . . . and it is NOT be the government's job. It goes completely against the principles in the Constitution.

Uh, Superfed, you can't do that.

Oh. Sorry.

With redistribution, some people start "expecting" the government to pay them for doing nothing. They start thinking it is their "right" to receive this money. Instead of being responsible for themselves and working hard, these people are encouraged to be lazy and irresponsible. Like the kite string, they've lost freedom to be self-reliant and to succeed.

 Dr. Franklin, didn't you write about this once?

 Yes, I did. I said, "I am for doing good to the poor, but I differ in opinion of the means. I think the best way of doing good to the poor, is not making them easy in poverty, but leading or driving them out of it. In my youth I travelled much, and I observed in different countries, that the more public provisions were made for the poor (welfare), the less they provided for themselves, and of course became poorer. And, on the contrary, the less was done for them, the more they did for themselves, and became richer."[28]

 Yeah . . . Government protects your right to TRY; it doesn't provide an EQUAL SUPPLY. ☺

Well said!

Side order of fries
that are all the same size

A Fairy Tale

Once upon the beginning of the school year, a teacher announced to the class:

> This semester, we are going to try something a little different. Instead of getting the grade you earn on each exam, everyone will receive the average of the total test scores. This way, you can all excel together as a class and you will all be equal. And no one will fail.

Reactions varied.

> But Mr. O, are you sure this is the best way to…

> Trust me, everything will work out best for everybody.

> Sweet.

After the first test, the grades were averaged and everyone got a B. The students who studied hard were upset. The students who studied very little were pleased.

> What?!?! But I earned an "A" on this.

> Sweet.

BIG GOVERNMENT

As the second test rolled around, the students who usually studied hard decided it wasn't worth it, so they studied less. Meanwhile, the students who studied very little didn't study at all this time. Why should they? The smart ones will carry the average.

The second test average was a C.

When the 3rd test rolled around, the average was a D. (Hmmmm, do you detect a pattern here?)

As the semester continued, the scores never increased. Normally diligent students stopped trying. What was the point? Their GPAs tanked, and so did their chances of getting into the best colleges. Meanwhile, normally lazy students got frustrated because those "selfish" smart students weren't trying anymore. No one would study for the benefit of anyone else. And the result was bickering, blaming, name-calling, and an overall feeling of frustration and hopelessness.

The Final Exam? F.

And they lived sadly ever after.

The End

The Moral of the Tale?

**When the reward is <u>great</u>, the effort to succeed is <u>great</u>.
But when someone takes all the reward away,
no one will try or want to succeed.**

Okay, so it wasn't a very happy tale.

But neither is the fairy tale notion that the inherently-flawed economic system called Socialism could actually bring prosperity to a nation.

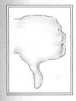

In SOCIALISM, as with this class of students, the people are supposed to work for the so-called "good of the country." Since they are not rewarded for their individual efforts, they lose their motivation to excel, to innovate, to work hard, and to produce. Laziness, mediocrity, and apathy take its place. Because of these attitudes, the government is unable to control and take care of its people (as it promised it would). Throughout history, socialism has always failed in the long run.

Compare that to the genius of the economic system called Capitalism.

In CAPITALISM, anyone has the freedom to excel based on his or her own efforts. People are motivated into action because they receive the rewards of their labors (kind of like the basketball tryouts analogy). They are not restricted by government policies and excessive taxes. There is optimism and hope for the future. Competition is encouraged, keeping prices down and inspiring innovation. Technology advances, the quality of life increases, and the nation as a whole prospers. Just think of the advancements the United States has a made in the past 200-plus years . . . largely due to capitalism!

And what's the government's job in all this? To control, take care of everyone, and make sure the wealth is distributed equally???

No! The government's job is to handle dishonest and criminal activity among businesses and corporations. That's it. Other than that, Government needs to just get out of the way! Let the PEOPLE build the economy and trust in the idea that CAPITALISM WORKS!

> Government protects your right to TRY (Capitalism),
> It doesn't provide an EQUAL SUPPLY (Socialism).

BIG GOVERNMENT

My dear young friends, there are many, many more things we could share regarding the problems of BIG government. We have just mentioned a few. For now, I think we've given you plenty to think about.

In conclusion, Let's take one last look at this second pyramid:

Here is

WHAT IS HAPPENING IN THIS NATION TODAY.

Now compare that with the first pyramid we discussed:

BIG GOVERNMENT

WHAT WAS INTENDED FOR THIS NATION BACK THEN

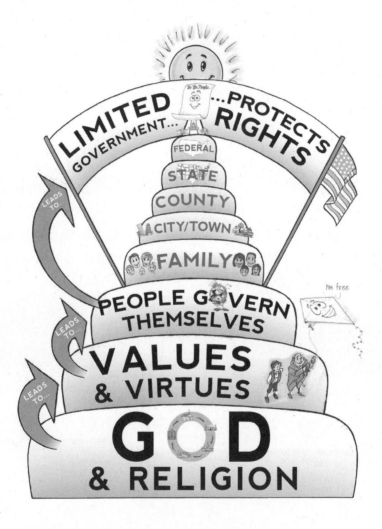

Now, Here comes the BIG question . . .

WHICH ONE LOOKS MORE STABLE TO YOU???

1)

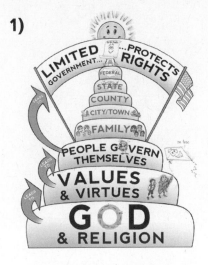

(It's a real toughie, I know.)

2)

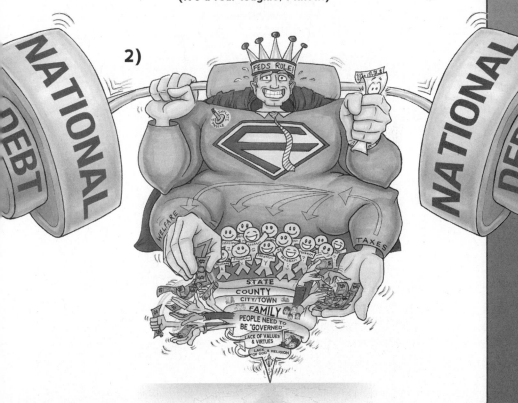

BOTTOM LINE: Sooner or later, Pyramid 2 will fall. It will not stand. If anyone thinks America can keep going the direction it is going and still maintain its greatness, they are just fooling themselves. How can it, when the very beliefs and values that made it great in the first place are, in large part, being ignored?

Wow. ☹ That's kinda scary. Really scary actually. So, what can WE do? I mean, we're still young. We can't even vote yet. How can we help get our country back to the original pyramid?

We were hoping you would ask that. What would you say, Mr. Washington?

I would say the best thing you can do while you are young is make Pyramid 1 represent **YOUR OWN LIFE**. Start with . . .

GOD & RELIGION. Grow closer to God. Attend church. Learn to pray. Read your Bible or whatever religious book your church has. Don't be afraid of these things or think they are "not cool." Like I said, we can't expect there to be morality in the country without religious principles. Your faith will help you learn the . . .

VALUES & VIRTUES we've been talking about. Be responsible. Be hardworking. Be generous. Be honest. Practice these values until they become habits. Learn other values & virtues. Make them a part of you, and you will have the freedom to . . .

GOVERN YOURSELF. Your parents will trust you. You will have more privileges. You will be happier. And when you grow older and it comes time to move out on your own, you won't need to be "controlled" or "taken care of" anymore by your parents. You won't have the entitlement disease. You will simply depend on a . . .

LIMITED GOVERNMENT to protect your rights. You will earn your own money. You will find your own place to live. You may go to college. You may start your own family. Your life will be whatever you make of it. But it will be your life. You will be independent!

Yeah. It's weird to think I'll be doing all those things someday . . . ya know, be old an' stuff.

I know, but it will happen sooner than you think. So, be ready for it.

Ha! I'm *still* waiting to grow up, my dear Mr. Washington!

 LOL ☺

My advice to you young people is . . . **LEARN.**
Just love learning!

Read good books. **Work hard** in school. **Be interested** in many things. I myself couldn't decide on just one thing to do in life, so I did many: inventor, scientist, statesman, diplomat, governor, public servant, philosopher, humorist, economist, printer, editor, publisher, athlete, writer, and even a musician (playing three different instruments). ☺

But in all your learning, continue to **learn about the founding of this blessed nation,** the United States of America. Learn what's in the Constitution! In your day, people are **NEEDED** who are educated in regards to that document.

It will take a lot of effort to reverse these problems we have talked about, but you can do it. And the knowledge you gain, even as a youth, will fuel your fire to **DO SOMETHING** about it as you get just a little bit older.

Mr. Madison, what about you? What counsel would you give?

Just as you said, Dr. Franklin. **DO SOMETHING** about it. Take the initiative and act!

At the risk of sounding boastful, I'd like to mention that the Constitutional Convention happened largely because I spoke up and **DID SOMETHING** about the problems I saw around me.

 Indeed.

 Hear, hear. James, explain to this younger generation what you did exactly . . .

 Well, we had just won our independence from England, but the country was a **mess**! We didn't have a federal government that could keep all the states united. The people in each state thought only about what was best for them. We were weak. Unless something changed, I knew we wouldn't last long as a nation. So I decided to **DO SOMETHING** about it.

I was young, small, and in poor health—but I didn't let that stop me. I took the initiative and invited all the state leaders together for the purpose of organizing a new national government. Some were eager to meet. Others were not. **But I kept at it**, refusing to take no for an answer.

Liberty Hall

After much effort, we, the leaders from all thirteen states, assembled in **Philadelphia**. It was the **summer of 1787**. For four hot, humid months we met in a stuffy building. I shared my ideas of how this new government could be organized. We discussed these ideas. We brought up concerns. We debated. We argued. We compromised. We came to agreement.

Finally, in September, **we signed the Constitution.**

All who were present knew that the creation of this Constitution was indeed a **miracle**.[29] At last, the states were united (the United States of America). We became one nation, under God, never to be divided.

My young Americans, that's how it works. It takes one person to stand up and **DO SOMETHING** for positive change to happen. You can't just wait around for someone else to do it. And when you stand boldly for truth . . . dozens, hundreds, thousands, millions will follow.

So who's going to stand up and **DO SOMETHING** in your time?

 I guess we will.

I speak for all of us "Founding Fathers" (as you call us) when we say, We pray you will.

We have given you knowledge. Now it's up to you to **DO SOMETHING** with it.

 We will! Thank you so much! This has been awesome!

 God bless you, my young Americans.

A FEW LAST THOUGHTS . . .

So, did you learn something? Was it "boring"? ☺

I've found that when you really start to grasp the principles and ideas that were the foundation of this nation, it makes you that much more **PROUD** to be an **AMERICAN**. Patriotism starts to mean a whole lot more than just saying the pledge of allegiance at school and flying the flag on the Fourth of July. It becomes a way of life. Even for young people!

To wrap things up, let's go back to the three facts we mentioned at the beginning of this book.

Three facts that every YOUNG American needs to realize...

 1) The United States of America was & is the greatest nation on Earth.

 2) Today, the United States of America is in serious trouble.

 3) You will inherit the USA—and its problems—in just a few short years.

When you first read those statements, it was probably a bit intimidating. Maybe even frightening. Or maybe you just didn't care.

Now, at the end of this book, you hopefully see those three facts in a whole new light. Instead of getting bummed-out or being apathetic, you're **motivated**! You're **excited**! Dude, you're **pumped**!

WHY are you pumped, you ask? Let me explain.

In his State of the Union address, James Madison once said:

> **"A well-instructed people alone can be permanently a free people."**

How so?

You have just been taught the principles and concepts that were at the foundation of this great nation—Pyramid I. You are now armed with that knowledge ("well-instructed" as Madison puts it). When you **ACT** on that knowledge, you will have the power to make choices that lead to freedom. You will be free to make decisions based on your faith and values. You will be free to govern yourself.

With this freedom, you will have the power to change things, to influence others, and to help **them** become "well-instructed."

You will compare what is happening around you politically to how it fits into the Constitution. You won't be deceived by governmental ideas that "sound" good, but that are not "soundly" based in the Constitution. You will look to that God-inspired document and the intent of the Founding Fathers as your guide.

You will get involved. You will talk to others about what you know. You won't keep silent. You will contact your elected government leaders about the issues, knowing it's their duty to represent **YOU**! You will demand accountability from them. You will vote. You might even become a government leader yourself. And you will pray for your country . . . because you will understand, as Benjamin Franklin did, **"that God governs in the affairs of men."**

That means we need God's help!

And when enough of you young, "well-instructed" patriots become free, you will restore this nation's foundational roots and become "permanently a free people." You will be a rising sun once more.

Now, don't be thinking this will be easy! It won't happen overnight. There has been **far** too much Pyramid 2 in our nation for **far** too long to expect this change to happen all at once. It will take time, patience, and persistent effort. It will involve staying focused on the end goal (a Pyramid 1 nation) and then taking steady steps to reach that goal.

Yes, it will be hard. BUT it can be done. It will be done. It **has** to be done. Millions of Americans are already striving in this effort to become "permanently a free people." The effort needs millions more. It needs everyone. Especially the next generation. It needs you.

Then, in time, we will need to add one more "fact" to the list:

FACT #4

And, under your stewardship, the United States of America will continue to be the greatest nation on Earth.

God Bless America!

REFERENCES

1 – Journal of the Constitutional Convention (17 September 1787).

2 – Speech to the Constitutional Convention (28 June 1787).

3 – *The Writings of George Washington*, ed. John C. Fitzpatrick (Washington: United States Government Printing Office, 1931-44) 30:292.

4 – Speech to the Constitutional Convention (28 June 1787).

5 – Ralph Ketcham, *James Madison* (Charlottesville: University Press of Virginia, 1990), 31.

6 – *The Writings of Benjamin Franklin*, ed. Albert Henry Smyth (New York: The Macmillan Company, 1905-07) 10:84.

7 – J. Randolph, *Early History of the University of Virginia* (1856), 96–97.

8 – Alexis de Tocqueville, *Democracy in America* (1840; New York: Vintage Books, 1945), 1:319.

9 – Ibid., 314.

10 – Ibid., 319.

11 – Ibid., 311.

12 – *The Works of John Adams* ed. Charles Francis Adams (Boston: Little, Brown and Company, 1850-56), 9:228-9

13 – "Articles of Belief and Acts of Religion" (1728).

14 – Benjamin Franklin, in a letter to his daughter, 1784.

15 – *The Writings of Benjamin Franklin*, 9:569.

16 – Russ Walton, *Biblical Principles of Importance to Godly Christians* (New Hampshire: Plymouth Foundation, 1984), 361.

17 – James Madison, Federalist No. 45, 292.

18 – The American Historical Review, vol. II, 618.

19 – Abraham Lincoln, A Proclamation, Oct. 3, 1863.

20 – *The Writings of James Madison*, ed. Gaillard Hunt (New York: G.P. Putnam, 1902), 1:460.

21 – *The Debates in the Several State Conventions on the Adoption of the Federal Constitution*, ed. Jonathan Elliot (Philadelphia: J.B. Lippincott, 1901) 3:536–37.

22 – Bernard Bailyn, "A Fear of Conspiracy Against Liberty" in *The American Revolution* (Boston: Little, Brown, 1971), 101.

23 – The Records of the Federal Convention of 1787, ed. Max Farrand, 2:641.

24 – Letter to Colonel Carrington (27 May 1788).

25 – *Writings of George Washington*, 32:211.

26 – Speech at the Virginia Convention to ratify the Federal Constitution (1788).

27 – First Inaugural Address, 1801.

28 – Benjamin Franklin, "On the Price of Corn and Management of the Poor," 29 November 1766.

29 – James Madison, Federalist No. 37, 230–31.

ABOUT THE AUTHOR

David Bowman's passion is teaching and working with youth. He has taught at a high school level and is a popular youth motivational speaker, traveling around the country to speak at various venues. David is the author/illustrator of several books for young audiences, including the best-selling Who's Your Hero series.

David is also passionate about restoring this nation back to its founding principles. Along with authoring this book, he is actively involved with the American Academy for Constitutional Education and other conservative groups. He, and his wife, Natalie, and their four children live in Arizona.

David Bowman has also produced a fine art series titled "Expressions of Christ."

To find links to David Bowman's

- "Expressions of Christ" fine art series
- "What Would the Founding Fathers Think" Blog
- Facebook & Twitter & More

go to www.davidbowmanonline.com.